The New Female Archetypes

Rethinking women's roles in groups through television

By
Jen Letherer

The New Female Archetypes: Rethinking women's roles in groups through television.

ISBN-13: 978-0692226032 (Supergirl Press)

Printed in USA by Createspace.

Cover design by Nicolas Cunningham
Cub Arcade https://www.facebook.com/cubarcade

Acknowledgements

My many thanks go to Wally Metts, for his encouragement and instruction. He is a visionary, a good shepherd, and a fan of Designing Women, which means I'm honored to be one of his mentees.

I also thank Jean Letherer (my very own mother) and Maggie Tibus (practically family as well) for doing their best to overcome my severe inability to copyedit my own writing. And it is to those two women, and all the fabulous women who have let me share their sewing circles, that I dedicate this book. You've taken them good, and taken them bad. Thank you for being my friends.

Table of Contents

"It proves what Jung said all along. Myths and archetypes are alive and well and living in my apartment." –Rose (Barbra Streisand) in The Mirror Has Two Faces.[1]

Chapter 1
Going Beyond Goddess and Femme Fatale

An archetype is a common personality pattern or type that is a representation of a naturally occurring social role. These more-than-stereotypes are the quintessential examples of characters' social functions. Everyone has to fit into the group somewhere, and these archetypes are roles we assume someone will naturally fall into in order to make the group function. Archetypes are the relationship tasks we either choose or are given based on how our social group functions.

Theorist Joseph Campbell wrote a lot about archetypes.[2] He detailed many different roles for men (like Hero, Father Figure, Mentor, Herald, Guardian, etc.) but noted only two major female archetypes, the **Goddess** and the **Temptress**. Other scholars have pointed out variations of the female roles, but none have settled into our collective consciousness in the same way. For years, females appearing onscreen have had to fit into one of these types. Women in movies, and on TV, were generally either one or the other, with little room in between.

The Goddess: The good girl. The Goddess is the mainstay of hearth, home, and reason. For instance, Olivia de Havilland in... well, all the movies she was ever in, including *Gone With the Wind* and *The Adventures of Robin Hood*. The quintessential TV example is Caroline "Ma" Ingalls (Karen Grassle) on *Little House on the Prairie*. Ma is always the voice of reason (unless one of her children is in danger), the baker of pies, and the dispenser of advice.

The Temptress: The bad girl. The Temptress in its most distilled form is the femme fatale, like Barbara Stanwyck in *Double Indemnity* or Sharon Stone in *Basic Instinct*. But it can also be the mean girl, after all Nellie Oleson (Alison Arngrim), the ultimate prairie witch,[3] did tempt all of Laura's boyfriends on *Little House.*

While there may be truth in these archetypal roles, many of those stories they appear in, and the theories about them, were written and shaped by men. In the latter part of the 20th Century and so far in the 21st, with a rise in the number of women working in mass media, mirroring the rise of women's rights and roles in the public sphere, these archetypes are worth a redefinition. Perhaps now that more women are working, and working in the entertainment industry, women are seen a different way.

An article by Lt. Colonel Prisco R. Hernandez[4] redraws the female archetypes (with the intent to formalize leadership roles) as Queen, Wise One, Faerie, and Lover. It's an interesting read... but if we dig into pop culture we might find them a bit antiquated. Updated, those four female archetypes might be called the **Leader**, the **Sarcastic Second**, the **Innocent**, and the **Flirt**: the one who holds the group together, the color commentary, the hopeful one, and the sexy one.

There are a number of films/stories with four women in main roles (and interestingly, a lot of them are set in the southern US). For example: *Steel Magnolias, The Divine Secrets of the YaYa Sisterhood, The Sisterhood of the Travelling Pants, Now and Then, Fried Green Tomatoes,* and the list goes on.

Women have also functioned in groups of four within a larger group story, and the group may shift and change as the story progresses. (*The Women, A League of Their Own, Meet Me in St. Louis*). In fact, in almost any movie where four named female characters exist, they take on these roles. For instance: in *White Christmas* the two major female roles are Betty (Rosemary Clooney) and Judy (Vera-Ellen). They are supported by the housekeeper, Emma (Mary Wickes), and the general's granddaughter Susan (Anne Whitfield). Betty, by virtue of ending up with Bing (Crosby, the film's leading male), is the leader of the group. Susan is obviously the Innocent. Judy, by all rights, should be the Sarcastic Second, but she's more of a Flirt, and Mary Wickes' brilliant turn as Emma makes her a fine Second. All roles are negotiable, but in the movies, on TV, and oddly enough in real life, they almost always balance out with all four profiles being present and identifiable.

But perhaps the group of four women is best illustrated by four different TV shows, all revolving around a primary group of four ladies, in which each of the women has a distinct role within the group. The following are four shows with four central female characters that gained popularity and ran at least six seasons: *The Golden Girls* (7 seasons, 1985-1992); *Designing Women* (7 seasons, 1986-1993); *The Facts of Life* (9 seasons, 1979-1988); and *Sex and the City* (6 seasons, 1998-2004).

Each of the women in these shows fit into the profiles of **Leader, Sarcastic Second, Flirt**, and **Innocent.** Each will be detailed in the following chapters. What's just as interesting is that if you assign personalities to the shows themselves (not just the women in them) this set of programs also fit the profiles:

The Golden Girls, headlined by the feminist likes of Bea Arthur and created by Susan Harris, is the unquestionable **Leader.** Not only do the characters have the qualification of maturity, but the creative team and sensitivity to timely social issues, as well as the awards won by the show (4 Golden Globes, 4 Emmys), set the bar for female group comedy. (For solo female sitcoms the *The Mary Tyler Moore Show* was the first critically acclaimed hit show that dealt with social issues with real female perspective. But notice how even then, the women function in similar roles. Rhoda is the quintessential sarcastic second.) Because of its comic depth and brilliant writing, it renegotiated the terms of women on Television as a force to be reckoned with. The women of *Golden Girls* had lived through it all, and Rose had the stories to prove it.

Designing Women was created by Linda Bloodoworth-Thomason. Like *Golden Girls*, it frequently wove social issues into its plot (rape, homosexuality, weight, beauty pageants, single parenthood, gun control, the list goes on), but also defended its identity as Southern. The 2-time Golden Globe (1 Emmy) winner dripped with sarcastic dialog, making it clearly the **Sarcastic Second**:

Suzanne Sugarbaker: I never use catalogs. I'd rather go in the store and see all the salespeople groveling and sucking up to you.
Julia Sugarbaker: Pardon me; I never knew they were so solicitous at the K-Mart.

The Facts of Life's young cast and popularity with younger viewers makes it the clear **Innocent**. While it dealt with social themes (disability, assault, body image), most of them were from the viewpoint of the teenage characters. As the show (and characters) matured, it lost steam, viewing audience, and sophistication. (What it gained, for negligible worth, was George Clooney.) It was probably never intended to be as sophisticated as the other shows, and its scripts are neither as precise nor clever. They are witty in their own right, and as will be seen, the appeal of the innocent is not in their naïveté, but their optimism. Besides, Jo and her motorcycle are the definition of chic cool, and empowerment. But if you're aiming less for badass and more for fabulous...

Sex and the City was created by Darren Starr, the man responsible for *Beverly Hills 90210* and *Melrose Place*. This alone qualifies the show as the **Flirt**. Of the four programs detailed, only *Sex and the City* deals centrally with relationships to the opposite sex. Heterosexual characters populate all of the shows, and many plotlines deal with romantic relationships. But *Golden Girls* is mainly about how the women live together; *Designing Women*, how they work together; and *The Facts of Life* how they grow up together. *Sex and the City* is indeed about sex, but it's really about relationships. So it's about how women navigate relationships with men (by talking with their girlfriends about them). Because of this, every episode deals with picking up, maintaining, or dropping (or being dropped by) the opposite sex. Since the Flirt is always aware of the appeal of the opposite sex, SATC couldn't fit the profile more.

So there they are, the **Leader, Sarcastic Second, Innocent,** and **Flirt.**

If the reader is still not convinced the archetypes are real, keep reading and see whether or not these roles being to become apparent in groups of women that populate our programs and our lives. They're everywhere, and these shows will illustrate just how the roles function within the re-sewn circles of sisterhood in our stories as well as our lives.

"Since the archetype of the Queen is the richest, most mature form of the Feminine, it cannot arrive at the pinnacle of life-enhancing majesty without first participating in the attributes of other important feminine archetypes." -Hernandez

Chapter 2
The Leader

The Golden Girls, Designing Women, The Facts of Life, and *Sex and the City:* each of these stories contains four major characters. But as is true with almost any story, if forced to choose, one can be singled out as the true main character. Without her the story could not truly continue. She's the center of the group, our proxy, the one with whom the audience feels the closest association, and the one who exerts the most influence on the groups' decisions.

The **Leader** of all feminine foursomes often carries the traits of other members of the group. She is often as witty and intelligent as the Sarcastic Second, as pretty as the Flirt, and as positive as the Innocent, depending upon the time and situation. But she's made leader for a number of reasons. Primarily, because the other members of the group look to her to make decisions, and because without her the group would disband, or at least not function as well.

In any group dynamic, one leader emerges. There may be a power struggle to establish it, but in a well-functioning group, there's a chain of command. For our feminine foursomes, it's not so much a chain of command as it is a chain of influence. And since each of these shows empowered women, and were socially progressive, the leader tends to be the spokesperson, especially concerning social views. One thing is certain: without her, the group wouldn't stay together. The Leader is given charge because she's the one who brings everyone into the circle.

Sex and the City: Carrie (Sarah Jessica Parker)

Carrie Bradshaw: As we speed along this endless road to the destination called Who We Hope To Be, I can't help but whine, 'Are we there yet?'

Probably the easiest leader to point out is Carrie Bradshaw. While all four NYC fashionistas get screen time, Carrie acts as narrator, and writes the column that serves as each show's "theme." We know about each of the girls' relationships, but Carrie's relationships with Big and Aidan get screen time that moves the plot of the show, and the arc of the series (as well as the movies). Carrie is the glue that holds the group together. She influences each of the characters, and in this case, even more tellingly, her character influenced audiences. According to Naomi Wolf of *The Guardian*, "Carrie Bradshaw did as much to shift the culture around certain women's issues as real-life female groundbreakers."[5]

Golden Girls: Dorothy (Beatrice Arthur)

She's not the oldest of the group, but she seems to have more of a handle on acting mature than her mother, who borrows money from her and is more apt to say the thing Dorothy might be thinking, but knows better than to say out loud. Dorothy also does not own the house; technically it belongs to Blanche. But Dorothy rules it. The audience consistently looks to Dorothy for common sense and answers. Dorothy is empowered and knowledgeable.

Kevin Kelly: Oh, no. You're not a substitute nurse too, are you?
Dorothy Petrillo-Zbornak: I'm sorry about your knee. You know, you wouldn't have been blindsided if you'd stayed in the pocket.
Kevin: You know football?
Dorothy: I know everything.

Dorothy freely admits she's made some poor choices. Like Carrie, her track record with men isn't a point of pride for her. In fact, that's probably why she's able to be the leader. The virtue of experience and gained insight means Dorothy is world-wise. She's not as innocent (clueless?) as Rose, nor as given to temptations of the flesh as Blanche. And she's still willing to lead, as opposed to Sophia, who is very passive about leadership. When Dorothy does get going, her opinions are well known. Dorothy is the only one of the four women to make serious comments on social issues. Beatrice Arthur became famous playing a related character, Maude Findlay, who was one of the most influential and outspoken women on TV in the 70's. Dorothy's liberal views are Maude's toned down and given a different context and goal. But Dorothy's reaction to situations says a lot about how women were and wanted to be represented in the media. And by watching Dorothy, the audience knows how to react to every situation: political, cultural, or otherwise. Just count how many reaction shots Bea Arthur gets each episode. We base our reactions on hers, and therefore she, too, leads the audience.

Designing Women: Julia (Dixie Carter)

Julia Sugarbaker not only owns and lives in the house which is the set for *Designing Women*, she's the boss of the company that calls it home (as proof, when she loses the house and ownership of the design firm in season six, she and Allison vie for the role of leader...and Allison loses; the audience doesn't side with her at all). We are, literally, always on Julia's turf. She, like Dorothy, has family around (her sister, Suzanne) and is perhaps even more well known for stating her opinions on subjects ranging from airline service to affirmative action. Throughout the show, characters wait for (or try to circumvent) opportunities to see Julia "fired up."

Suzanne Sugarbaker: I'm serious, Julia. I do not want you to get up on your soapbox about this one. Otherwise, I might have to point out to everyone that you own a fur coat yourself. You know what I'm referring to.

Whether she's telling off the bigoted or simply expressing frustration, Julia's rants are the payoffs. She too holds the audience's reactions. Julia's speeches are rhetoric acts that, for instance, reclaim insults to women:

Charlene Frazier Stillfield: What'd they say?
Julia: Who?
Charlene: The adolescent cretins.
Julia: It doesn't matter what they said. They said what they always say.
Charlene: Well I know, but just out of curiosity, what was it?
Julia: All right, Charlene. If you must know, they said, 'Say, Mama, sure would like to be your Daddy. Mmm Mmm got to have me some of that.'

Or act as catharsis against bigotry and judgment to, for instance, those who would claim that AIDS is a "gay" disease:

Julia: Imogene, I'm terribly sorry. I'm gonna have to ask you to move your car.
Imogene Salinger: Why?

Julia: (pulling her towards the door) Because you're leaving. The only thing worse than all these people who never had any morals before AIDS are all you holier-than-thou types who think you're exempt from getting it... ... Imogene, get serious! Who do you think you're talking to? I've known you for 27 years, and all I can say is... if God was giving out sexually transmitted diseases to people as a punishment for sinning, that you would be at the free clinic all the time! ... and so would the rest of us!

Julia is a mouthpiece, yes, but with muscle. She represents the group, and directs what it does, as well as how. The others acknowledge that she takes responsibility for the group. Even if she didn't want to be, the others would nominate her group leader. Julia doesn't shy away from that responsibility, she openly acknowledges it. Since the others, for the most part, agree with her, she's the leader and spokesperson for their group, and the main reason they all stick together.

The Facts of Life: Jo (Nancy McKeon)

Jo Polniaczek: There are people in this world who get shoved around and there are people who do the shoving!

Jo is probably the hardest leader to pin down, but that's because she's indicative of the archetype. It's Jo who really holds the group together. The first season of *The Facts of Life* was a set up, a primitive stage. The program and Charlotte Rae were still cutting their ties to *Diff'rent Strokes*, and the cast contained 7-8 women in major roles. The foursome was not established until the first episode of season 2, when Jo's character was introduced. As an outsider, Jo needed to make connections with all the characters. Natalie and Tootie were given more screen time than in the first season, and Jo was pitted from the very start against her rival, Blair.

Jo Polniaczek: (to Blair) Do you hear yourself, or do you just talk?

Blair could be the group's leader. She is charismatic, and takes initiative. Both Natalie and Tootie are passive (reinforced in almost every episode; they consistently copy the older girls). She is a person of great influence. Which is why, when she meets Jo, she sees her immediately as a rival. Blair may have money and social graces, but Jo is world-wise and active.

Jo is a reluctant leader, but becomes one by virtue of being different: she's from New York and is unfazed by men, alcohol, or hot-wiring vehicles. Her tomboyish-ness makes her the antithesis of Blair's femininity. Jo's difference initiates change. At a private all-girls school, someone mechanical, sarcastic, and aggressive is bound to be a trendsetter. Jo initiates change, and when she does, Natalie and Tootie follow. It also goads Blair into keeping up. Their friendship/rivalry will drive the show in terms of plot, as well as attitude. And who does the audience side with? More often than not, it's with the common-sense (although hot-headed) opinions of Jo.

It's almost as if Blair initiates rivalry with Jo so that Jo will take on the leadership role, and Blair can resume being superficial. It's because of Jo and Blair contesting who knows more about men that the four girls end up in jail and wrecking the school van. These events lead to them working for Mrs. Garrett and rooming together. So, Jo is the one who puts the four of them in the same room and is therefore, again, responsible for giving the group cohesion.

So what traits do the four **Leaders** share?
Influence: They change the way other members of the group think or behave. Quite often, people look up to them as role models in the group of four.
Social Action: They speak seriously (sometimes to comic effect. Okay, often to comic effect) about serious issues. Because these are feminine, progressive programs, quite often they tackle issues for women and other under-represented groups.
Audience Alignment: They elicit the most sympathy or insight from the audience.
Group Decisions: In the end, they speak for the group.
Involvement: Without them, the group doesn't stick together.

Now, think about a group of four women you know. Is there not a leader who fits this description? They may be witty and intelligent. But because they have to lead, they may not always be able to say whatever is on their mind. That job, or the job of being the "smart one" then falls to: the **Sarcastic Second.**

Chapter 3
The Sarcastic Second

According to combined histories of dueling, "At the field of honor, each side would bring a doctor and **seconds**. The seconds would try to reconcile the parties by acting as go-betweens to attempt to settle the dispute with an apology or restitution. If reconciliation succeeded, all parties considered the dispute to be honorably settled, and went home. Each side would have at least one second; three was the traditional number."[6]

Traditionally, when there was a formal fight to be had, part of the code of honor was that combatants brought their own backup to act as both mediator and potentially to continue the fight on the dueler's behalf.

The members of each female foursome need that kind of solidarity. But as backup for what? Since each of the shows have socially progressive plotlines, especially for women, it is backup for rhetorical opinion. But because the shows are personal stories and those personal stories matter more than agendas, it's also backup for life. The groups are groups of friends. The battle is getting through life together.

Very seldom in these groups is there one pair of self-proclaimed best friends. Instead the relationships ebb and flow over time, and the group is a group of besties. Sometimes more pronounced than others, though, there is one person who, when the Leader is absent, becomes the default leader or is seen as the leader's right hand, their Second. Quite often, that person is known specifically for intelligence, artistry, and wit. They follow the Leader by adding knowledge, softened with humor. They are often neurotic, self-conscious, and incredibly sarcastic. **The Sarcastic Second** is the essence of both solidarity and wit.

Designing Women: Mary Jo Shively (Annie Potts)

If Julia drives Designing Women, Mary Jo rides shotgun. She's often described as feisty, and she can be (see season three's "Big Haas and Little Falsie"), but her sarcasm is put to use in wit, in cleverness. Mary Jo could easily be the innocent, but she's too smart for it. When she's not backing up (or enjoying) Julia's rants, she's speaking her mind in her own way. As is often the case, the Leader sets the tone and the subject matter and the Second is the comic muse. Mary Jo's answer is usually not to rant (she's too passive, which is why she's not the Leader) but to be clever, self-depreciating, and sarcastic.

Mary Jo Shively: I was too embarrassed to tell you...
James Dean 'J.D.' Shackelford: Tell me what?

Mary Jo: I have never had sex with anyone but Ted.
J.D.: You haven't?
Mary Jo: And I do not know anything about anyone else. I mean, Ted's idea of foreplay was holding me by the feet and saying, 'Make a wish.'

Her wit is backed up by intelligence. Julia is cultured and educated, but Mary Jo is the trained interior designer. She's the artist, the one who does the sketches and color matching. She's the antithesis of Suzanne, who concentrates on appearances. Shallow is one thing Mary Jo can't be, even when she tries. Mary Jo is also the one who doesn't fly off the handle, but gets the job done, for instance, in the season three episode "Oh What a Feeling" when the other three women (and Anthony) are all unable to talk to a car salesman and get a good deal. While they plot revenge in the powder room, Mary Jo calmly walks in and points out the extra charges on the sales sheet, refusing to pay them. She avers that she knows how to do this because she was forced to learn price negotiations while living in Mexico with her (now ex) husband. Quite often, the Second is as independent as she is intelligent, and has overcome enough to stand on her own.

The Facts of Life: Natalie Green (Mindy Cohn)

Natalie Green: Who wants to be a skinny pencil? I'm happy being a magic marker!

Jo's sarcasm is a defense mechanism because she's aggressive; Natalie's wisecracks are a defense mechanism because she's clever and wants to lighten the mood. When the situation gets tense, Natalie can use self-depreciation to lighten the mood and remind everyone not to take the situation so seriously. This is her defense against criticism (I'll point out my own flaws so someone else can't) and her offense against tension (If I poke fun at myself and get everyone laughing, the mood will lighten). Tootie's wit is precocious; Natalie's is charming. She's an academic leader among leaders (editor of the school paper), and as unpretentious as it gets. Like Mary Jo, she relies on self-depreciation because she's so smart, and because she's actually dealing with her own self-confidence (and dealing with it in a pretty healthy way as the show continues).

Natalie is perhaps the most approachable of all the characters. She doesn't come from the designer label life of Blair, and she doesn't have the gritty self-reliance of Jo's New York. Mrs. Garrett is older so there's less audience alignment; Tootie is naïve, and viewers connect with people who have more insight). Nat's acceptance of her own foibles added to her open manner would be effective on their own. But Mindy Cohn's brilliant delivery of one-liners (often smiling at her own jokes) makes Natalie the wise, neurotic, intelligent, and funny one.

Tootie Ramsey: Skinny dipping. Won't it be a little cold for that?

Natalie: So we'll wear gloves!

The Golden Girls: Sophia Petrillo (Estelle Getty)

Dorothy Petrillo-Zbornak: Ma, why do you continue to take pleasure in amusing yourself at my expense?
Sophia Petrillo: Because we don't have cable and I can't crochet. This is who I am Dorothy, either learn to live with it or have me medicated.

Sophia is entirely capable of being a Leader, but she earned the right to ask her daughter for money, crack jokes about aging kidneys, and say exactly what she thinks. Sophia also uses humor to diffuse situations and makes jokes about her own flaws.

Sophia: I'd offer you one of my kidneys but I think you'd rather have one you can control.

She supports Dorothy when she needs a lift, and keeps her humble by embarrassing her daughter whenever possible. Dorothy, as the leader, always wins because Sophia depends upon her for physical needs (and she threatens Sophia with Shady Pines). But Sophia doesn't let Dorothy's aggressive nature get the best of her, and she keeps the mood light. She's too wise (and too experienced) to be the innocent, and would be the flirt if age and Catholicism didn't stand in her way. Like Natalie, she can be counted on for one-liners. She's also the best backup money can buy.

Sex and the City: Miranda (Cynthia Nixon)

Like Mary Jo, Miranda is the intellectual professional. She's a successful female lawyer, made partner by season three. Her independence is assertive. She's not as fashion conscience as either Samantha or Carrie, and she's not as determined to be in a relationship as Charlotte. Miranda's wit and intellect are her saving grace and her fatal flaw. Like Sophia, she says exactly what's on her mind. Like Natalie, she uses humor to diffuse her self-consciousness. *Sex and the City*, the movie, is the distillation, the essence of all the characters. The series had come to an end, and the characters' roles were firmly established. In the film, the story had only two hours to make people's relationships mean just as much as they had over six television seasons, so each of their actions had more meaning. In the film, while all the ladies comfort Carrie after she's jilted, it's Miranda who is single with her (it was also partly Miranda's doing that she got jilted). It's Miranda that Carrie gets mad at, and it's Miranda she forgives so she can forgive Big. Miranda is Carrie's backup because she, too, has a myriad of flaws.

Understanding Miranda is hard, unless you know someone like her, or are like her yourself. Then she becomes an open book. She's the one who has to have it all together (especially when she really doesn't), who can make snarky comments with the best of them, who always has her wits about her and wears them as a mantle and a medal. She's self-depreciating, introverted, and clever. But she's a mom, too (in Miranda's case, the only one with a child on the show). Most **Sarcastic Seconds** are deeply sensitive people, just like most **Flirts** are deeply intelligent people but have to concentrate on image to get by socially and most **Innocents** are quite wise, but come across as foolish because they are so adamantly optimistic. Just as neither the Innocent is as clueless nor the Flirt as shallow as she may seem, the Second is in some ways never as tough as she looks but in others more tough than maybe even she gives herself credit for.

The Sarcastic Second is usually the hardest to identify. Quite often it happens by default. But common traits abound: **independence, intelligence, self-depreciation and humor as defense.** When her sarcasm gets the best of her, the Sarcastic Second can get a bit cynical. When that happens, the group turns to the **Innocent.**

Chapter 4
The Innocent

Lt. Hernandez' list of female archetypes: Queen, Wise One, Lover, and Faerie, describes the Faerie as "...*not just a Princess, she is the symbol of all that is fair, all that is beautiful, all that transcends material existence."* She is someone with virtue, untainted and untouched. The prize the warrior strives after. She's a lady trapped in a tower, or sleeping after pricking her finger, or waiting for Robin Hood to rescue her from Prince John. She is a passive object, there only to serve as a pawn in the real hero's plot. That's the ideal faerie of a woman: the innocent goddess.

That, of course, is not a real woman, though. If she does exist, it's an oversimplification at best. Real women may be beautiful and fair, but if they are only the objects of affection, then they aren't people, they're just objects. The Faerie Princess is an objectification. Respect is one thing and virtue is always to be commended. But to assume that women have but *one* virtue is a pretty narrow view of the feminine species. If the **Flirt** is the absence or rejection of being identified solely on the basis of sexual virtue, the **Innocent** is generally the one who accepts this virtue, and strives to meet it. You will notice that our Innocents may not have the cleanest sheets in the world, but among their female foursomes, they are the most concerned with virtues of abstinence. They are generally the most passive, and often either the youngest, the most naïve, or both.

While this naïveté is often portrayed negatively (our shows deal with active, not dependent women), the Innocent's worth is still imperative. For one, she balances out the Flirt. For another, her inexperience, inhibition, or ignorance is on occasion the saving grace of a situation. And finally, the Innocent is also the foil for the Sarcastic Second, because she is neither as world-weary nor as cynical. She is eternally hopeful. That's her role in the group. If the Innocent loses hope, the group's ability to function becomes nearly nonexistent.

The Golden Girls: Rose Nylund (Betty White)

Rose Nylund: Can I ask a dumb question?
Dorothy Petrillo-Zbornak: Better than anybody I know.

Rose's leading characteristic as the Innocent is her cluelessness. She is not as sharp witted as Dorothy, and does not feign dementia like Sophia. Rose is the classic definition of the wise fool. She may seem unable to lead and as dysfunctional as a Second but when Rose is taken seriously, her wisdom is unparalleled. She is untainted by cynicism. And sometimes, her unplanned wit and honesty are more succinct because she does not try.

Rose: *We should put out the welcome mat.*
Blanche Devereaux: *We don't have a welcome mat.*
Rose: *What about the one Dorothy always says is at the foot of your bed?*

But if there's one area in which Rose truly shines, it's in seemingly useless but truly entertaining information. Rose is a treasure trove of stories. Pointless? Occasionally. Self-depreciating? Often. Worthwhile? Good heavens, yes.

Rose: *Let me tell you about a lesson that I learned when I was a little girl in St.Olaf. If you hold a bird gently, the bird will stay. But if you squeeze the bird, his eyes will bug out. And Mr. Petshop Owner won't let you touch the birds anymore.*

The Facts of Life: Tootie Ramsey (Kim Fields)

If *The Facts of Life* is about growing up, Tootie is the child who wants to be taken seriously. Like Rose, she is often cast off as unable to understand or comprehend. Her friends often try to shield her from experience (which never works) so she can remain the Innocent. But the series is also about crossing social divides (see Blair and Jo) and Tootie has experience in this area. Why? She's an African American at a pricy

East-Coast boarding school in the early 1980's, something the show didn't make an issue of, but also did not ignore[8].

Blair Warner: Come on, slave week is supposed to be fun. Just think you buy an upper classman and she's your slave for three whole days!
Tootie Ramsey: Blair this may come as a shock to you, but slavery is not one of my favorite things.

The *Facts of Life* was a spinoff of *Diff'rent Strokes*, which also had a precocious young black actor who was world wise but wholly innocent. In fact, Gary Coleman made several guest appearances on *The Facts of Life,* in which he pursued Tootie romantically, to comic effect. This is one of his Arnold character's stock and trade gags: the adorable cad. But unlike Arnold, Tootie does not assume she is mature to cover blatant immaturity. Tootie aspires to maturity, and grows by experience. She keeps a diary, wears roller skates, and adores Michael Jackson. She and Natalie are both inexperienced, but Tootie also takes on the quality of being more hopeful, more childlike and less tongue-in-cheek sarcastic. She is often straightforward and honest. And by being so, keeps the others in check (see the infamous pillow fight episode in season four as one example).

Designing Women: Charlene Frazier Stillfield (Jean Smart).

Like Rose, Charlene is clueless. Like Tootie, she is inexperienced. And like both, she is kind, sweet, and more fun than a bridal shower with an oldies lip sync[7].

Charlene Stillfield: [Referring to condoms] I remember my Daddy used to keep a whole bunch of them in his top dresser drawer. I got in so much trouble once 'cause I blew them all up on my birthday. I mean I was real confused about the facts of life. One time my parents were out of town and I crashed my bicycle into this wall and I couldn't find a Band-aid. I showed up at school the next day with a Kotex taped to my forehead.

Charlene: At our house it was kind of a zoo with eleven kids at Thanksgiving.
Suzanne Sugarbaker: What was that like having a hillbilly Thanksgiving? Did you have Turkey?
Charlene: (sarcastically) No. Possum! Daddy killed it, Mama stuffed it, then at the table we'd all have a big food fight, then afterward whittle sticks and sit on the front porch pickin' our teeth!
Suzanne: Ok ok... I was just asking.
Charlene: Well you're always just asking! I curse the day I ever told you we had an outhouse.

Charlene's innocence is not to be confused with a lack of intelligence. She comes from (and often references) a simpler experience, a romantic view of the past (see any of the episodes relating to her relationship with Bill), and a heart untainted by mistrust. Of the crew at Sugarbaker's, Charlene is the only unmarried one when the show premieres, and after she meets and marries Col. Bill Stillfield (Douglas Barr), she remains with him through the run of the series. She is traditional without being backward, demure without ulterior motive, and passive without being a pushover. She begs a friend to leave an abusive husband, attends church and sees a psychic, and can find the good in anyone. She still loves Elvis. She is hope eternal. If called for, Charlene could be a leader. But this would not serve the group best. What they need is someone to remind them there is good in people and beauty in nostalgia.

Sex and the City: Charlotte York (Kristin Davis)

While the Innocent may seem inhibited:

Charlotte York: Wait a second! I thought you were serious about this guy; you can't sleep with him on the first date.
Samantha Jones: Oh, god!
Miranda Hobbes: Here she goes again with 'The Rules.'

Perhaps it is also true that those who seek virtue obtain stability and happiness.

Samantha: Relationships aren't just about being happy. I mean, how often are you happy in your relationship?
Charlotte: Every day.
Samantha: Every day?
Charlotte: Well, not all day every day but yes, every day.

Charlotte is either the most inhibited, or the most virtuous of her friends, depending on your point of view. Like Charlene, she seeks a traditional marriage and family. Also like her fellow Innocents, she is the most inexperienced. Throughout the show, Charlotte is introduced to various sexual experiences her friends have already tried. She is the first to get married, but not the first in a long-term relationship (and her first marriage doesn't last as long as several of those relationships, notably Carrie and Big, Carrie and Aidan, and Miranda and Steve). Charlotte loves sex as much as any girl (except maybe Samantha, and who can compete with that?) and she is promiscuous. But almost as proof that our perceptions of moral standards (which can be very different than standards themselves) are arbitrary, Charlotte is piqued by conscience more often than the others when it comes to bedroom behavior.

Nowhere is this more obvious than in the season three episode "Frenemies," in which Charlotte and Samantha have a falling out over the subject of sexual conversations and behavior. While Samantha finds someone with even fewer inhibitions than her own, Charlotte has lunch with her college sorority sisters. Both are outside their true group of best friends. Charlotte sits at lunch with a different group of women (another foursome). With Carrie, Miranda, and Sam, Charlotte's role is defined. She wears preppy outfits, goes through bride magazines by the dozen, and gets excited about things that seem lame to the other three. With her Greek girls, Charlotte starts talking about sex, and realized that in this group, she's the obvious Flirt. So much so that the other women ask her to leave. Charlotte can be who she is with her foremost foursome. Her role suits her. She fits there. Charlotte is a Flirt to the uptown sorority set, and it doesn't feel natural to her. With Carrie, Miranda, and Sam, she can be the Innocent one, and that fits her best. That's a person she can be happy being.

The **Innocent** is **inexperienced** so audience members can be unintimidated. She is **hopeful** in order to make harsh social realities more palatable. She is the **child at heart** so the others can be grown up, and **clueless** so the others can be wise. The burden of virtue is not heavily born by the Innocent. They are absolved of the duties of wisdom and experience, and child-like enough to make their friends and their audience remember the good things around them. Sometimes, though, the rules of social norms need to be challenged, and the girls ready to step in and make a stand are the ones ideally suited to objectify men in the same way the media has objectified women for years. Those women are the **Flirts.**

Chapter 5
The Flirt

There's one in every group. In grade school, she's the one with the pretty ribbons, dresses and the nicest Barbie dolls. In high school she's the first one with cleavage (or the first one to flaunt it). She's the one who you never feel quite as safe having your boyfriend/brother/trusted-guy-friend-who-isn't-gay talk to. As she ages, she only reminds you more and more of Mae West.

Some **Flirts** are born, some are made, and some have libidos thrust upon them. That should probably be restated: some people just have Flirty stages.

And not all Flirts are obsessed with sex. In general, the leading characteristics of a Flirt are that she is very concerned with outward appearances and holds fewer inhibitions when it comes to the opposite sex. All the archetypes under discussion play out in real life. Television versions are often, as is the case with most stories, heightened or exaggerated examples. So the Flirts we known were probably not that promiscuous. Okay, not all of them. But almost assuredly, they liked to look fabulous.

Sex and the City: Samantha Jones (Kim Cattrall).

Samantha Jones: Practically all the relationships I know are based on a foundation of lies and mutually accepted delusion.

Samantha: I'm a trisexual. I'll try anything once.

Samantha is not just a **Flirt**; she's a sexual free agent. She does not have sex to raise her own self-esteem. She does not attract men because she never had a good relationship with her father. She just loves sex, and knows she can get it. Nowhere is this more apparent than in her most long-term relationships, where she gives up sex (or good sex), at least for a time, in order to make the relationship work. She is the essence of empowering female sexuality. Samantha calls the shots in the bedroom (or fire station, or wherever) and does what pleases her. Study any female depictions in the media (and consult anything written by Laura Mulvey, Molly Haskell, or Jeanine Basinger) and you see that women are consistently used as sexual objects by men, for men's pleasure. All of *Sex and the City* revolves instead around female pleasure. Samantha is the essence of this. Her promiscuity is not about using people or force. It's about women getting to do what men have done for centuries: use sexual promiscuity as a way to command their own lives and their own pleasures. Samantha makes no excuses nor carries any outside motives. She does not dress to please the opposite sex; she dresses to entice them on her own terms. Hello, her name is fabulous.

Golden Girls: **Blanche Deveraux (Rue McClanahan).**

Blanche Devereaux: I swear as God is my witness I will never pick up another man... in a library... on a Saturday... unless he's cute... and drives a nice car... Amen.

Samantha and Blanche share a great deal in common. Perhaps the most important is that they are promiscuous and not twenty. The ability of men to "play the field at any age" is rampantly addressed in pop culture criticism (see any discussion on Sean Connery, George Clooney or Michael Douglas). Blanche and Samantha prove that sexy doesn't stop at forty. Or fifty. Or ever. (Side note: Betty White has since picked up the mantle of "sexy at any age," and done so with incredible flair.) Also like Samantha, Blanche is not an airhead. She's smart, but driven by an (over?) active libido. This in itself is revolutionary. Samantha is premenopausal. Blanche is not. All the women on *Golden Girls* are empowered: Dorothy is socially empowered because she intimidates, well, everyone. Sophia is because she's not senile. She speaks for an under-represented nursing home population. And she laughs about this, which is really powerful. Rose is empowering because she truly cares. She may seem clueless, but has incredible wisdom couched in her eternal optimism. But Blanche does something incredibly vital. For centuries men ruled the bedroom. Blanche, before Samantha, made it a place where women could call the shots, and have their own way.

Blanche: Ah, look at the shameless way she's flirtin' with him.
Rose Nylund: You flirted with him.
Blanche: I'm from the South. Flirting is part of my heritage.
Rose: What do you mean?
Dorothy Zbornak: Her mother was a slut, too.

Blanche accepts the term slut, not as an insult, but as a reclaimed moniker. The other women make reference to her being a "slut" fairly often. Now, say what you will about the decline of moral virtue, etc., etc., but this show aired in the 1980's, when casual sex became a socially acceptable norm. In an age when the senior generation could easily be forgotten, Blanche is the epitome of the idea that we are who we are even when we become members of AARP, and that inhibitions placed by society or ourselves are always negotiable. Agree with her behavior or don't, but understand she represents freedom that only men and young people had in our society.

Designing Women: Suzanne Sugarbaker (Delta Burke).

Julia Sugarbaker: Suzanne, if sex were fast food, there'd be an arch over your bed!

Suzanne is promiscuous (she's been married four times and throughout the run of the show dates a string of very old, very rich men) but she's also a beauty queen. Literally. Throughout the series, references to Suzanne's stint as Miss Georgia are made, and develop plot lines. Her defining characteristics are being shallow and self-indulgent. She's not stupid, she just doesn't care enough about things she sees as trivial. Like political correctness (see the ep. titled "There's Some Black People Coming Over for Dinner.") Or politeness (see any episode.) Or anything that detracts the universe from revolving around her.

Appearances are incredibly important to Suzanne. That's why her job at Sugarbaker's is to find clients. Social networking is her specialty, because she's a Flirt. In her culture, business and pleasure can both be achieved by a visit to the country club. (Why not? Men do it all the time.) Suzanne is, of course, not nearly as shallow as she comes off. No Flirt is. Each Flirt has their psychology discussed on some level during the show. We always know that behind the emphasis on looks there's a person who is achieving a sense of self. Blanche and Samantha are pretty well adjusted in this area. Delta Burke's brilliant turn as Suzanne is funny, charming, and quirky (embodied by her pet pig, Noel, which was a gift from her housekeeper Consuela). It is also an exercise in self-exploration. When Suzanne does show her real heart, we see it is as big as anyone's. And once that's established, she can comfortably slip back into the role of the one who is concerned about looks, money, dating, and being high society, so the rest of the group doesn't have to.

The Facts of Life: Blair Warner (Lisa Whelchel).

Blair Warner: I have natural ability.
Jo Polniaczek: Sometimes that's not enough.
Blair: It is when your natural ability is being rich.

Shallow? Yes. Concerned about appearances? Yes. Spends a great deal of time attracting the opposite sex? Yes. Like Samantha, she is a fashionista. But she's much more related to Suzanne. Both are beauty queens (Blair is Eastland Harvest Queen three years running). Both come from money and want to keep it that way. Both are concerned with family lines and public image.

Tootie Ramsey: [Tootie is asking everyone to teach her to drive] Blair?
Blair: I'd love to Tootie, if only I didn't have a fear of Volkswagens.
Natalie Green: You have a fear of Volkswagens?
Blair: That I'll be seen in one.

Like Suzanne, Blair's shallowness is a cover for unhappiness. Her compensation for everything is that she is smart, rich, and beautiful. Point: notice how all

Flirts use beauty as power. They've gotten ahead on their looks. So looks are incredibly important.

Natalie: Blair, how would you feel if men sat around all day rating you?
Blair: I'd love it.
Tootie: But it's so de-humanizing.
Blair: Not when you're a 10.

And like her fellow beauty queen, Blair has a distinct air of say-what-you-think-ness.

Blair: [Walks in to where Tootie is auditioning for a Broadway play] My look at all these unemployed people.

The role of the **Flirt** is to **release inhibition** and reclaim the **power** women have always had socially. By being **fabulous,** the Flirt gets attention. By being **assertive**, the Flirt is her own woman. The roles of women throughout history have been negotiated around power. Both sexes are intelligent. Men, in general, have brute strength. Women's physical prowess has historically been centered on beauty, on surface appeal. The Flirt can't be the leader because she would have to show restraint for the good of the group. She's a release for everyone. Her physicality is her defense and her offense, and when open society takes offense, they must choose to love her or leave her. But they cannot ignore her. There's a lot to say on this subject, but perhaps the endnote should be given to Samantha, for saying what may be true of all women:

"When I'm good, I'm very good. But when I'm bad I'm even better." Well that's just fabulous.

Chapter 6
Balance: The Sewing Circle

Marlene Deitrich may have given the sewing circle a new connotation (detailed, with questionable credentials, by Axel Madsen in *The Sewing Circle: Hollywood's Greatest Secret: Female Stars Who Loved Other Women*) but women bonding in groups is nothing new, nor does it necessarily connote lesbianism. (Although it might. That's not these shows, nor these groups, though.)

Throughout history, when women work in groups their work was not just with their hands, but also with their minds and hearts. They did, and still do this, by conversation.

My mother tells me that when she was first married and my Aunt Mary would drop by to visit, Mom would stop what she was doing, sit down, and chat. Aunt Mary was…a conversationalist…to say the least, and Mom would end up with unfinished tasks. So one day when Aunt Mary came over, Mom didn't stop folding laundry. Instead, she said, "Mary, could you fold these towels?" and went to load more things in the washer. Aunt Mary didn't skip a beat, but kept on chatting. Soon, the laundry was done, and Mom was caught up on neighborhood news.

The function of the female foursome is friendship. This includes managing life and work and men and, yes, gossip. None of the shows under discussion are plot driven. They are, as most sitcoms are, character driven. Character and relationship development are what the show is really about. And these friendships develop while they work away at life.

The Golden Girls' theme song is about friendship in longevity, and the senior señoras of Miami do work together fairly often. They are a social group, and a family. Their sewing circle no longer needs work to keep the four women in the same place, nor an excuse for four women to spend that much time together.

Designing Women: The workingwomen at Sugarbaker's are the essence of Aunt Mary-ness and the sewing circle. As they go about their work (professional in this case, not a quilting bee) they discuss their lives, society, religion, children, men worth dating, construction workers making cat calls, the First Amendment, breast implants, and race relations.

The Facts of Life: Jo, Blair, Natalie and Tootie go through an after school special every week. What's more high school than spending time talking through drama with your friends? The four of them work together in

Eastland's dining hall (and later for Mrs. Garrett's pastry shop, etc.). They are always having conversations while clearing dishes, cooking, and doing homework.

Sex and the City: The girls talk to each other throughout their working day as well as in their down time, and brunch discussion always centers around men. While each have careers, their real work in the series is the work of relationships, and through all of Carrie's frustrations with Big, she keeps coming back to what she can really depend upon, her friends. Writing about men is Carrie's day job. So, those conversations are a big part of her life and her work. The girls and their boys, and the conversations about them, make up Carrie's career, so in a sense whenever they have these discussions they are "working together" in more ways than one.

The women of *Sex and the City* choose to spend time together outside of work. In fact, all of the groups develop past needing the excuse of work to spend time together. This, too, happens in real life. And if women naturally fall into these archetypal roles, then women are constantly seeking the group where they fit best at home, at work, or in any social group. When they find a place where they really fit, they have found a group with true solidarity, maintained and preserved because the women depend upon it.

The group needs a **Leader** so there is someone to set the tone and ultimately make decisions. She's also often a role model for the others, even if she does not intend to be. She holds them together, and has the *je ne se quoi* that gives the group a heart, as well as hands.

Because the Leader has to make decisions for the good of the group, she needs a **Sarcastic Second** to help advise and inform her, to lighten the situation with wit, and to expose foibles inherent in all humans. The Second is necessary so we can laugh at ourselves.

When the Leader becomes too tired of leading, the Second too cynical, and the Flirt too disappointed and empty, the **Innocent** steps in to bring back hope. If it is true that "He that increases knowledge increases sorrow" (Ecclesiastes 1:18) then perhaps it is true that, "She who is active and advances social change increases in frustration and cynicism." Those who still see beauty in simplicity, or have not sacrificed ideals while taking comfort in tradition, restore hope. Those who see the good are encouragers. Their faith is powerful.

The **Flirt** acts on impulse, and loves to indulge. She is shallow and beautiful. There is probably a little of this in every woman, and in order to not act on it, we do so vicariously through our friend the Flirt. She can function as the Flirt because she has the group to remind her that she is more than all these shallow things. And so knowing, continues to go shopping... for men.

I say all of this as someone who was an Innocent growing up, but whose best fit is a Sarcastic Second.

There are two pictures on display in my house of three college buddies and I from our time at Siena Heights University in Michigan. My friend "K" was our natural leader. She shared in-jokes with everyone. She was a quiet leader, but cared for the group because she honestly loved us, and we her. My friend "Y" was the Innocent. I'm not sure if that role is her best fit, but at the time, she fell into it naturally. "D" and "V" (one is in each picture) were both and still are wonderful friends, and socialized with the group in different contexts. But both also had a flair for clothes and, well, for one it was Justin Timberlake.

Perhaps why those college relationships felt so right is because we could be ourselves. I'm neurotic and self-conscious, an honor student, and like to think I'm funny. So the Sarcastic Second felt like a natural place to be. I liked the role, and still do. My college girlfriends and I still talk, but time and geography make us unable to be the *Sex in the City* girls. That's natural, I think, and in no way detracts from how much fun we had or what we meant and mean to each other.

What things break up a group? Miscommunication and misunderstanding, of course. Career choices (and the geography that goes with them: see Samantha's later plotlines, or Jo's absence from the last *Facts of Life* reunion) at times. Most often: men. When one or more of the women get married, the group must adjust. You'll notice that in each of the shows, a serious romantic relationship threatens group relations unless the lady consciously makes her girlfriends a major priority.

Perhaps single women need sewing circles. This conversation and sense of family are safe, encouraging, and give life a sense of purpose. When one belongs, one knows who she is. Romantic love can often become self-centered. Philial "friendship" love can be too, but not in the same way, or with the same consequences. Men may betray her, but the girls never will. Or let me re-phrase that: relationships with men are one to one, and intimate in other ways, so betrayal is very personal, and feels total. But with many girlfriends, even a betrayal is not total. We depend upon our girlfriends for a different kind of love and acceptance than we do from the opposite sex. There is less ownership of the other and more meeting with the group on one's own terms.

In many ways, we learn the basics of relationships with our friends, so we can put them into practice in romance, when the stakes feel much higher. And when romance fails us, we go back to those we learned and grew with. At least, that's what plays out on Television. Does it reflect real life or is it a structure of understanding that heightens life by putting it in story form? I guess that's up to the viewer to decide.

Notes

Streisand, Barbara, prod., dir. *The Mirror Has Two Faces*. Tristar Pictures, 1996. Film.

[2] Campbell, Joseph. *The Hero With a Thousand Faces.* Princeton, NJ: Princeton UP. 1968.

[3] Arngrim's autobiography is titled *Confessions of a Prairie Bitch.*

[4] Prisco R. Hernández. "Jung's Archetypes as Sources for Female Leadership," Kravis Leadership Institute, *Leadership Review*, Vol. 9, Spring 2009, pp. 49-59.

[5] Wolf, Naomi. "Carrie Bradshaw: Icons of the Decade." *The Guardian*. 21 December 2009. Web. 12 March 2014. <<www.theguardian.com/world/2009/dec/22/carrie-bradshaw-icons-of-decade>>

[6] Wilson, John Lyde. *The Code of Honor*. Ebook. Web. 7 March, 2014. <<http://www.gutenberg.org/files/6085/6085-h/6085-h.htm>>

[7] Like the one her friends throw for Charlene in Season 3, Episode 18's "Come on and Marry Me, Bill."

[8] Fields would go on to star in *Living Single*, another show with four female leads, this time with a predominantly African American cast. On that program she is most decidedly the Flirt.

Quotes and show references from:

Designing Women: Seasons 1-7. Linda Bloodworth
    Thomason, creator. Originally produced by Bloodworth-
    Thomason, Columbia Pictures Television, and Mozark
    Productions. Distributed by Shout Factory, 2009-2012.
    DVD.

The Facts of Life: Seasons 1-5. Dirs. Jim Drake, John Bowab, Nick
    Havinga. Originally produced by Embassy Pictures and TAT
    Communications Company. Distributed by Sony Pictures
    Home Entertainment, 2006. DVD.

The Golden Girls: Seasons 1-7. Originally produced by
    Touchstone Television and Witt/Thomas/Harris
    Productions. Distributed by Buena Vista Home
    Entertainment, 2004-2007. DVD.

Sex and the City. Dir. Michael Patrick King. Perf. Sarah
    Jessica Parker, Kim Cattral, Cynthia Nixon, Kristin Davis.
    New Line Cinema, 2008. Film.

Sex and the City: Seasons 1-6. Created by Darren Star.
    Originally Produced by Darren Star Productions, Home
    Box Office and Sex and the City Productions. Distributed
    by Home Box Office Video, 2000-2004. DVD.

www.ingramcontent.com/pod-product-compliance
Lightning Source LLC
Chambersburg PA
CBHW071342290326
41933CB00040B/2090